Queen Angelfish

by Julie Murray

Abdo Kids
ROYAL ANIMALS

Abdo Kids Jumbo is an Imprint of Abdo Kids
abdobooks.com

abdobooks.com

Published by Abdo Kids, a division of ABDO, P.O. Box 398166, Minneapolis, Minnesota 55439.

Printed in the United States of America, North Mankato, Minnesota.

102024

012025

THIS BOOK CONTAINS
RECYCLED MATERIALS

Photo Credits: Alamy, Getty Images, Minden Pictures, Shutterstock

Production Contributors: Teddy Borth, Jennie Forsberg, Grace Hansen
Design Contributors: Candice Keimig, Pakou Moua

Library of Congress Control Number: 2024936624

Publisher's Cataloging-in-Publication Data

Names: Murray, Julie, author.

Title: Queen angelfish / by Julie Murray

Description: Minneapolis, Minnesota : Abdo Kids, 2025 | Series: Royal animals | Includes online resources and index.

Identifiers: ISBN 9798384903017 (lib. bdg.) | ISBN 9798384903710 (ebook) | ISBN 9798384904069 (Read-to-me ebook)

Subjects: LCSH: Marine angelfishes--Juvenile literature. | Fishes--Juvenile literature. | Aquatic animals--Juvenile literature. | Animal kingdom--Juvenile literature.

Classification: DDC 597.58--dc23

Table of Contents

Queen Angelfish

The queen angelfish is found in the warm waters of the western Atlantic Ocean. It lives in **coral reefs**.

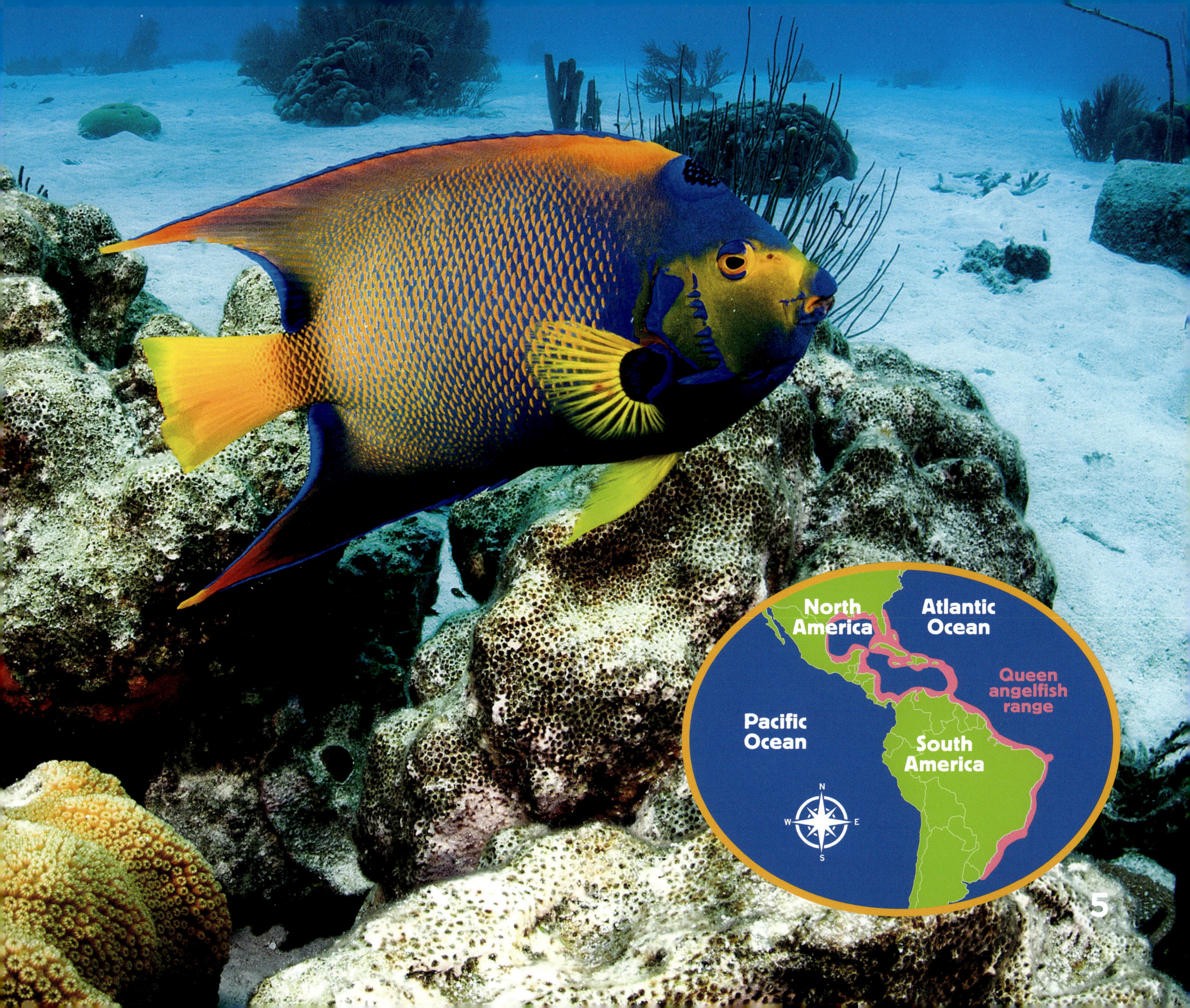

North America
Atlantic Ocean
Queen angelfish range
Pacific Ocean
South America
N
W
E
S

The queen angelfish never swims too far from the **coral reef**. It is found living alone or in pairs.

Its royal name comes from the speckled blue ring on its head. The marking looks like a crown that a queen wears.

Body

The queen angelfish has a flattened, oval-shaped body. It can grow up to 18 inches (45.7 cm) long. It can weigh up to 3.5 pounds (1.6 kg).

It is a very colorful fish! It has a blue body and a bright yellow tail. It also has light orange and purple coloring.

Camouflage

The queen angelfish's vibrant colors act as **camouflage**. The fish blends in with colorful **coral reefs**. This helps it hide from **predators**.

Food

Adult queen angelfish mainly eat **sponges**. Sponges make up more than 90% of their diet! They also eat **algae**, coral, and jellyfish.

Sponge
Jellyfish

Baby Queen Angelfish

Queen angelfish eggs are **fertilized** in open water. The eggs float until they hatch into **larvae**.

Larvae continue to grow and settle on the bottom of the reef. Young queen angelfish get their bright colors as they grow.

More Facts

- Queen angelfish are also known as blue angelfish, golden angelfish, and yellow angelfish.
- Their average lifespan in the wild is 15 years.
- Young queen angelfish feed by eating loose scales and other things off of larger fish.

Glossary

algae – organisms that live mainly in the water and make their food through photosynthesis.

camouflage – a way of hiding something by covering or coloring it so that it looks like its surroundings.

coral reef – a structure that rises up from the bottom of the sea and is made up of the hard skeletons of tiny sea animals called corals. Coral reefs are found in warm, shallow sea waters around the world.

fertilized – to have made or produced eggs.

larva – an animal after it hatches from an egg and before it changes into its adult form.

predator – an animal that hunts other animals for food.

sponge – a sea animal that has a body with many small holes or channels that water can flow through.

Index